Cecilia McDowall

Da Vinci Requiem

vocal score

for soprano and baritone soloists, SATB chorus, and orchestra

MUSIC DEPARTMENT

OXFORD

UNIVERSITY PRESS

OXFORD
UNIVERSITY PRESS

Great Clarendon Street, Oxford OX2 6DP,
United Kingdom

Oxford University Press is a department of the University of Oxford.
It furthers the University's objective of excellence in research, scholarship,
and education by publishing worldwide. Oxford is a registered trade mark of
Oxford University Press in the UK and in certain other countries

First published 2019

Impression: 2

ISBN 978-0-19-351902-2

Music and text origination by Katie Johnston

Printed in Great Britain on acid-free paper by
Halstan & Co. Ltd, Amersham, Bucks.

Contents

Duration: 35 minutes

Movement three, 'I obey thee, O Lord (*Lacrimosa*)', may be performed as an individual anthem and is available separately for purchase (ISBN 978–0–19–352905–2).

Composer's note

Da Vinci Requiem

La Prospettiva de' perdimenti (The Perspective of Disappearance)

I have brought together my chosen Latin texts for this Requiem with extracts from The Notebooks of Leonardo da Vinci, editions of which have been in my family for over seventy years. Leonardo da Vinci's extraordinary philosophical writings cast reflective and penetrating insights into the nature of mortality and all that it encompasses. The Requiem, structured in seven movements, advances from a dark, contemplative opening to hopeful luminosity in the final movement, 'Lux aeterna'. In the closing bars all voices drift upwards, folding into silence, an allusion to Leonardo's concept of 'The Perspective of Disappearance'.

'*The human bird shall take his first flight, filling the world with amazement, all writings with his fame, and bringing eternal glory to the nest whence he sprang.*'—Leonardo da Vinci.

Commissioned by Wimbledon Choral Society and its music director Neil Ferris to mark its centenary.

First performed at the Royal Festival Hall, Southbank Centre, London, England, by Wimbledon Choral Society, Philharmonia Orchestra, Kate Royal (soprano), Roderick Williams (baritone), and conductor Neil Ferris on 7 May 2019 to resonate with the 500th anniversary of Leonardo da Vinci's death.

This note may be reproduced as required for programme notes.

Instrumentation

2 flutes (doubling piccolo)
2 oboes (doubling cor anglais)
2 clarinets in B flat (doubling bass clarinet)
2 bassoons (doubling contrabassoon)
2 horns in F
2 trumpets in B flat
timpani
percussion (glockenspiel, suspended cymbal, side drum, tambourine, vibraphone)
harp
strings

Full scores, vocal scores, and instrumental parts are available on hire/rental from the publisher's Hire Library or appropriate agent.

If required, the work may also be accompanied by piano, playing from the vocal score.

Texts and translations

The Latin texts are from the *Missa pro defunctis*, with an English translation shown here in italic type. Unless otherwise stated, the English texts are by Leonardo da Vinci (1452–1519), taken from '*The Notebooks of Leonardo da Vinci*: arranged, rendered into English, and Introduced by Edward MacCurdy' (Jonathan Cape, London, 4th impression, 1945).

1. Introit and Kyrie

Requiem aeternam dona eis, Domine,	*Eternal rest give unto them, O Lord,*
et lux perpetua luceat eis.	*and let perpetual light shine upon them.*
Te decet hymnus, Deus, in Sion,	*A hymn, O God, becometh thee in Sion,*
et tibi reddetur votum in Jerusalem:	*and a vow shall be paid to thee in Jerusalem:*
exaudi orationem meam, ad te omnis caro veniet.	*hear my prayer; all flesh shall come to thee.*
Requiem aeternam dona eis, Domine;	*Eternal rest give unto them, O Lord,*
et lux perpetua luceat eis.	*and let perpetual light shine upon them.*

O Leonardo, why do you toil so much? (Windsor 12700 and Codice Atlantico, 71r)
Because movement will cease before we are weary of being useful. (Aphorisms, 685)
Shadow is not the absence of light: merely the obstruction of luminous rays by an opaque body.
(Ms 2038, Bibliothèque Nationale, 22r)
We are all exiled living within the frame of a strange picture. (attrib. L d V)

Kyrie eleison. Christe eleison. Kyrie eleison.	*Lord, have mercy. Christ, have mercy. Lord, have mercy.*

2. The Virgin of the Rocks

Mother, is this the darkness of the end,
The Shadow of Death? And is that outer sea
Infinite imminent Eternity?
And does the death-pang by man's seed sustained
In Time's each instant cause thy face to bend
Its silent prayer upon the Son, while He
Blesses the dead with His hand silently
To His long day which hours no more offend?
Mother of grace, the pass is difficult,
Keen as these rocks, and the bewildered souls
Throng it like echoes, blindly shuddering through.
Thy name, O Lord, each spirit's voice extols,
Whose peace abides in the dark avenue
Amid the bitterness of things occult.

For 'Our Lady of the Rocks', by Leonardo da Vinci
Dante Gabriel Rossetti (1828–82)

3. I obey thee, O Lord (*Lacrimosa*)

I obey thee, O Lord, first because of the love which I ought to bear thee: secondly, because thou knowest how to shorten or prolong the lives of men. (Foster III. 20 v.)

Tears come from the heart, not from the brain. Our body is subject to heaven, and heaven is subject to the spirit. (Tr. 65 a)

Lacrimosa dies illa,	*Full of tears will be that day*
Qua resurget ex favilla	*When from the ashes shall arise*
Judicandus homo reus.	*The guilty man to be judged;*
Huic ergo parce Deus:	*Therefore spare him, O God:*
Pie Jesu Domine, dona eis requiem. Amen.	*Merciful Lord Jesus, grant them eternal rest. Amen.*

4. Sanctus and Benedictus

Sanctus, sanctus, sanctus Dominus Deus Sabaoth.	*Holy, holy, holy Lord God of Hosts.*
Pleni sunt caeli et terra gloria tua.	*Heaven and earth are full of thy glory.*
Hosanna in excelsis.	*Hosanna in the highest.*

Benedictus qui venit in nomine Domini.	*Blessed is he who cometh in the name of the Lord.*
Hosanna in excelsis.	*Hosanna in the highest.*

5. Agnus Dei

Agnus Dei, qui tollis peccata mundi,	*Lamb of God, that takest away the sins of the world,*
dona eis requiem, sempiternam requiem.	*grant them rest, eternal rest.*

One sees the supreme instance of humility in the lamb. (Bestiary, Codice H:11 r)

6. O you who are asleep

O you who are asleep, what thing is sleep? Sleep resembles death.

Ah, why then do you not work in such a way that after death you might resemble yet a perfect life, when, during life, you are in sleep so like the hapless dead? (Codice Atlantico 76, v. a)

What is it that is much desired by men, but which they know not while possessing? It is sleep.
   (L d V Notebooks 1 56 [8] r)

Since a well-spent day makes you happy to sleep, so a well-used life makes you happy to die. (Codice Trivulziano 28 a)

7. Lux aeterna

Lux aeterna luceat eis, Domine:
cum sanctis tuis in aeternum,
quia pius es.
Requiem aeternam dona eis, Domine,
et lux perpetua luceat eis:
cum sanctis tuis in aeternum,
quia pius es.

May light eternal shine upon them, O Lord,
with thy saints for ever,
for thou art merciful.
Eternal rest give to them, O Lord,
and let perpetual light shine upon them:
with thy saints for ever,
for thou art merciful.

Once you have tasted flight, you will forever walk the earth with your eyes turned skyward, for there you have been, and there you will always long to return. (attrib. L d V) O Leonardo.

Requiem aeternam dona eis, Domine,
et lux perpetua luceat eis.

Eternal rest give to them, O Lord,
and let perpetual light shine upon them.

Commissioned by Wimbledon Choral Society and its music director Neil Ferris to mark its centenary.

In loving memory of Helly Bliss and for all those who grieve.

'If the Lord, who is the light of all things, vouchsafe to enlighten me, I will treat of Light.'—Leonardo da Vinci

DA VINCI REQUIEM

La Prospettiva de' perdimenti (The Perspective of Disappearance)

1. Introit and Kyrie

Missa pro defunctis
The Notebooks of Leonardo da Vinci (1452–1519)

CECILIA McDOWALL

2. *The Virgin of the Rocks*

Dante Gabriel Rossetti (1828–82)

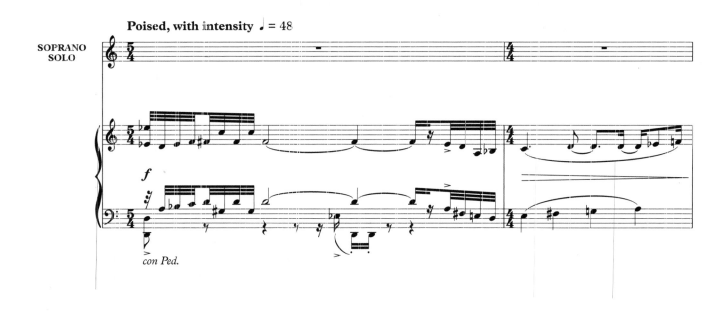

Mo-ther of grace, the pass is dif-fi-cult,

D

Keen

as these rocks, and the be-wil - dered souls Throng it like e - choes, e - choes,

blind - ly shud-der-ing through, shud-der-ing through.

E

44

Thy

47

name, O Lord, each spi - rit's voice ex - tols, Whose

50

peace a-bides in the dark av-en - ue A - mid the bit-ter-ness, the bit-ter-ness of things

53

oc - cult.

3. I obey thee, O Lord (Lacrimosa)

Missa pro defunctis
The Notebooks of Leonardo da Vinci (1452–1519)

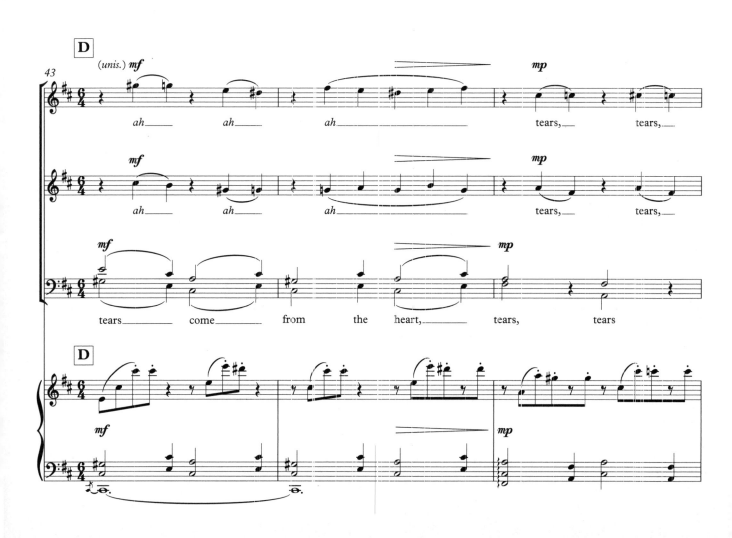

4. Sanctus and Benedictus

Missa pro defunctis

26

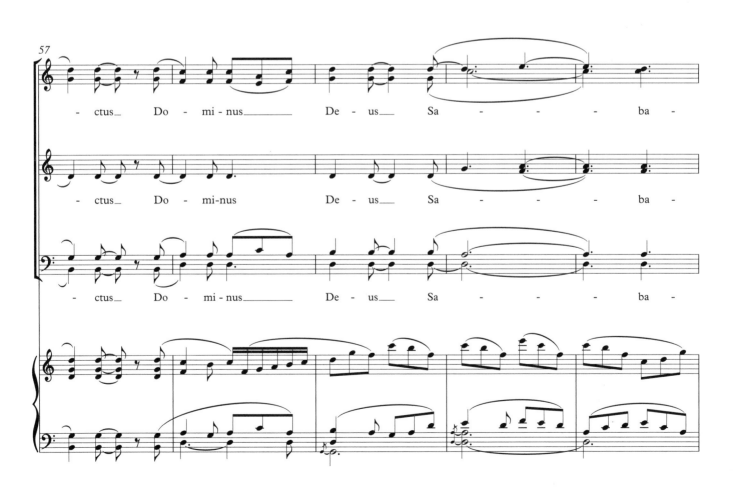

5. *Agnus Dei*

Missa pro defunctis
The Notebooks of Leonardo da Vinci (1452–1519)

★ The solo may be sung by the baritone soloist or by a tenor or bass soloist from the chorus.

40

6. O you who are asleep

The Notebooks of Leonardo da Vinci (1452–1519)

50

then _____ do you not _____ work in such a way that af - ter death _____ you might re-

-sem - ble yet _____ a per - fect life, _____

when, dur - ing life, _____

_____ you are in sleep _____ so like the hap - less dead? _____ You are in

pochiss. rit.   a tempo

while pos-sess - ing?   It___ is sleep,

it___ is sleep.

BAR. SOLO

Since_____ a well-spent day makes you hap-py_____ to sleep,_____

so a well - used_____ life_____ makes you

hap - py, hap - py to die._____

7. Lux aeterna

Missa pro defunctis
The Notebooks of Leonardo da Vinci (1452–1519)

* Cue-sized notes for rehearsal only.

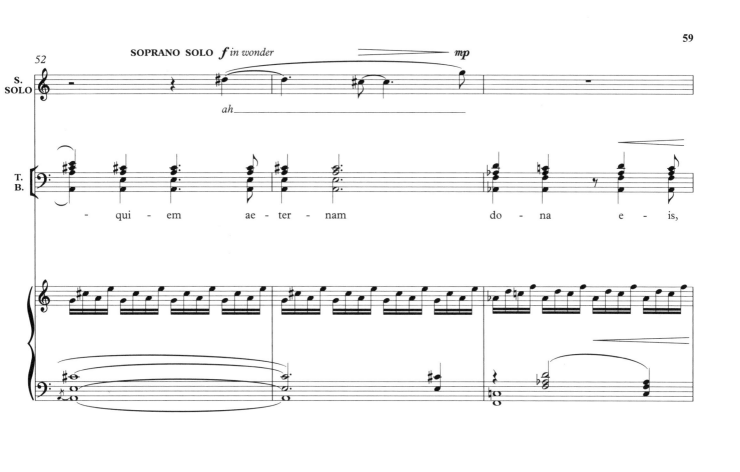

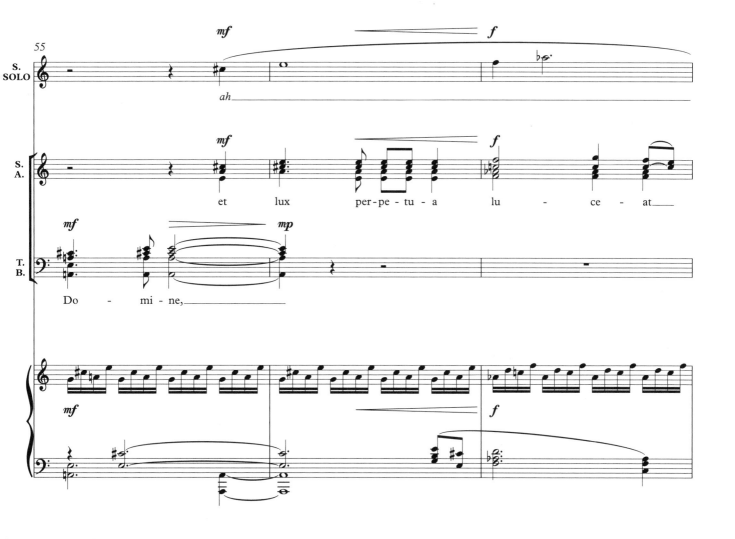

*Vocal glisses are optional in bars 66–81.

62

La Prospettiva de' perdimenti (The Perspective of Disappearance)